MW01644432

Aa

Apple

Bb
Butternut
Squash

Cc Cantaloupe

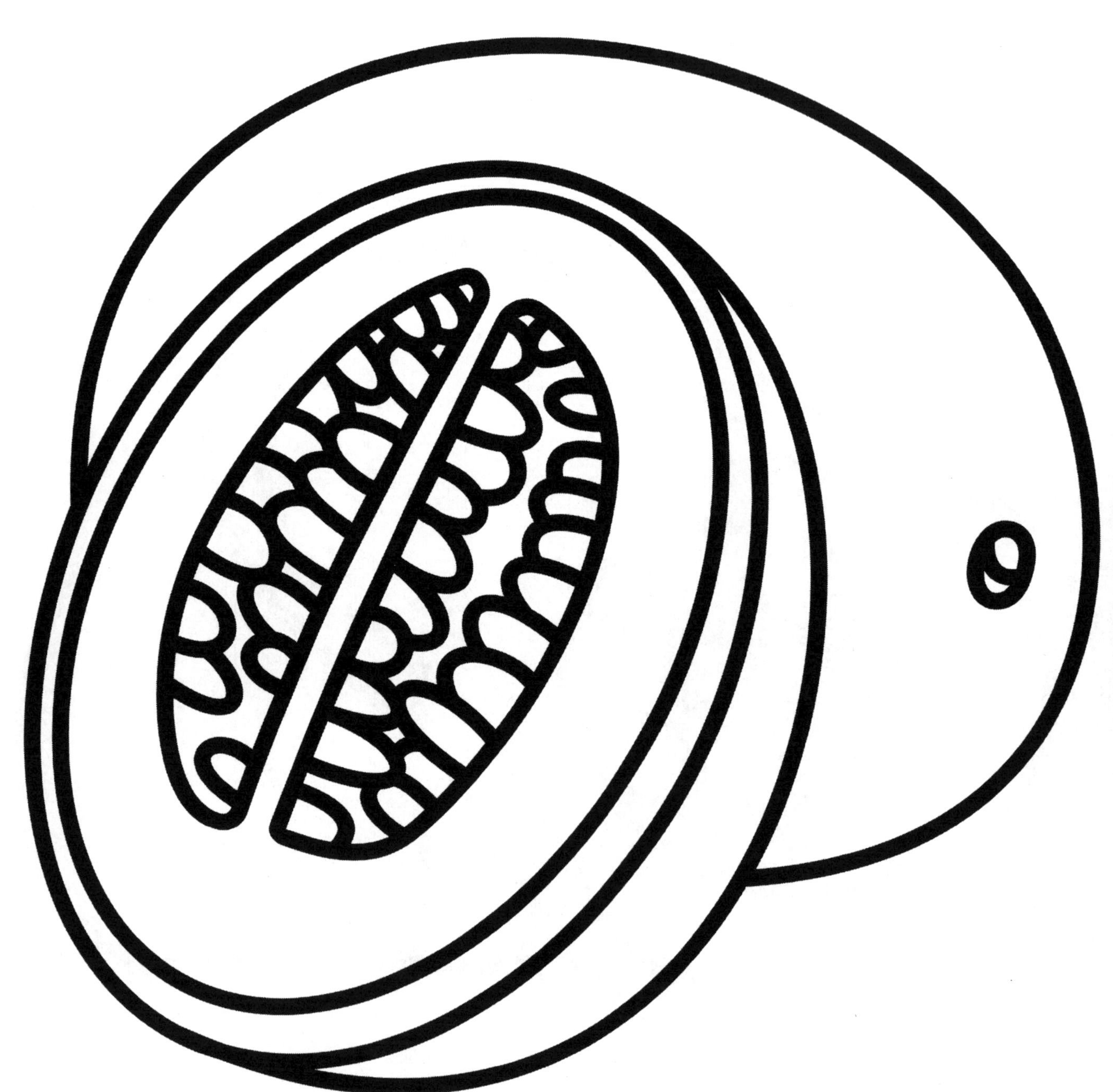

Dd
Dates

Ee
Elderflower Tea

Ff
Figs

Gg

Ginger

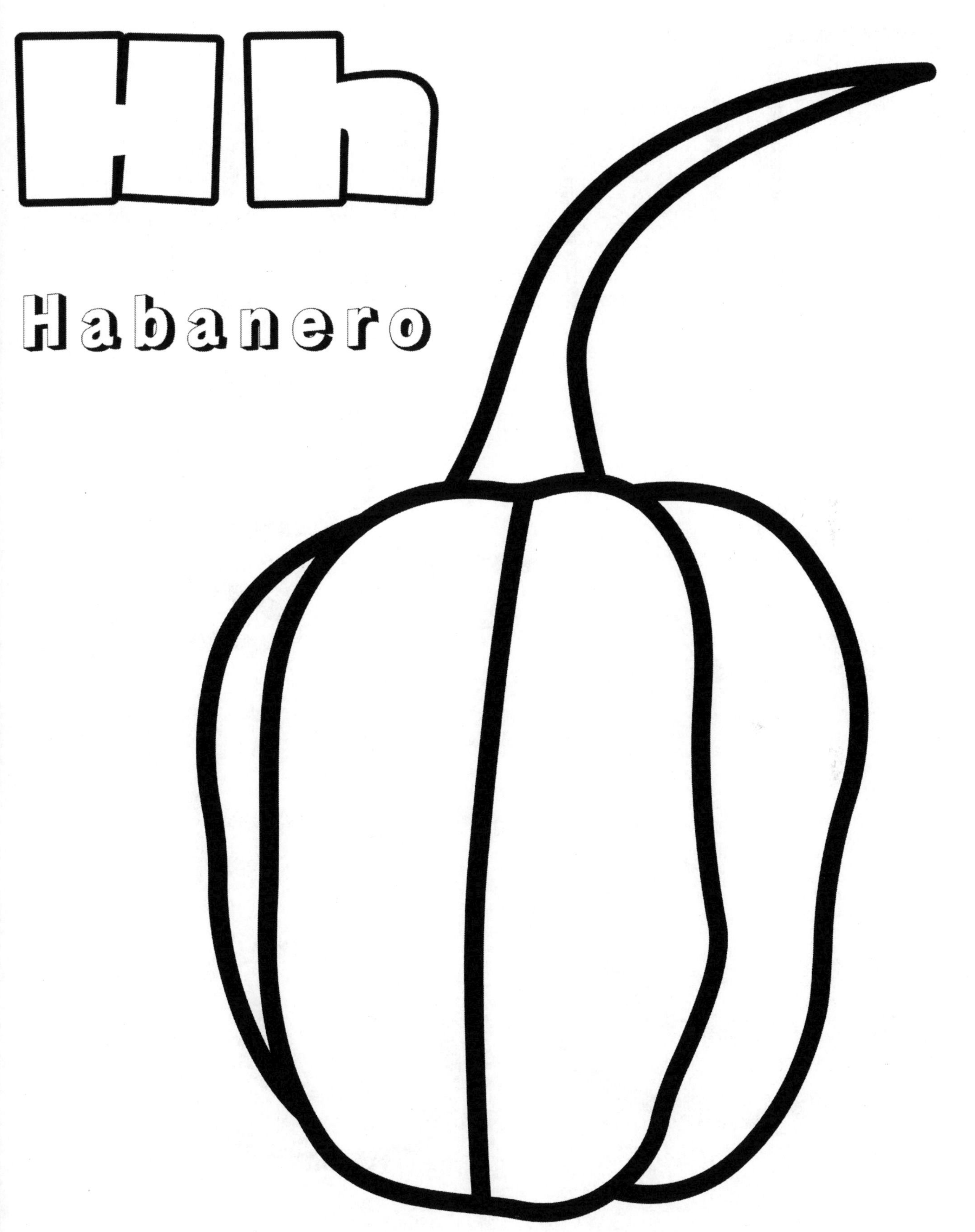
H h
Habanero

Ii
Iron

Jj
Juicer

Kk
Kale

L l
Love

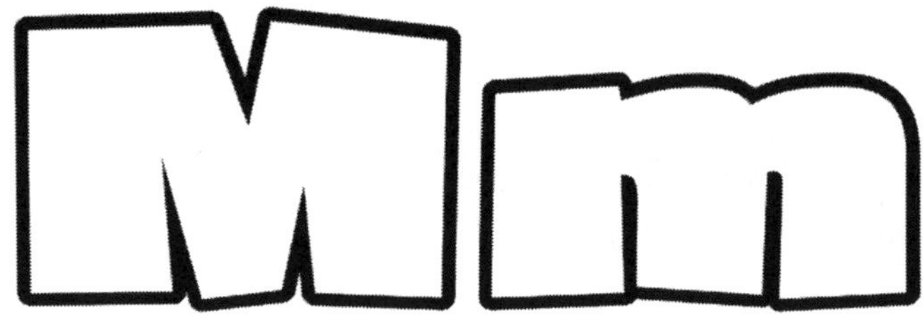

Mushroom
(Portobello)

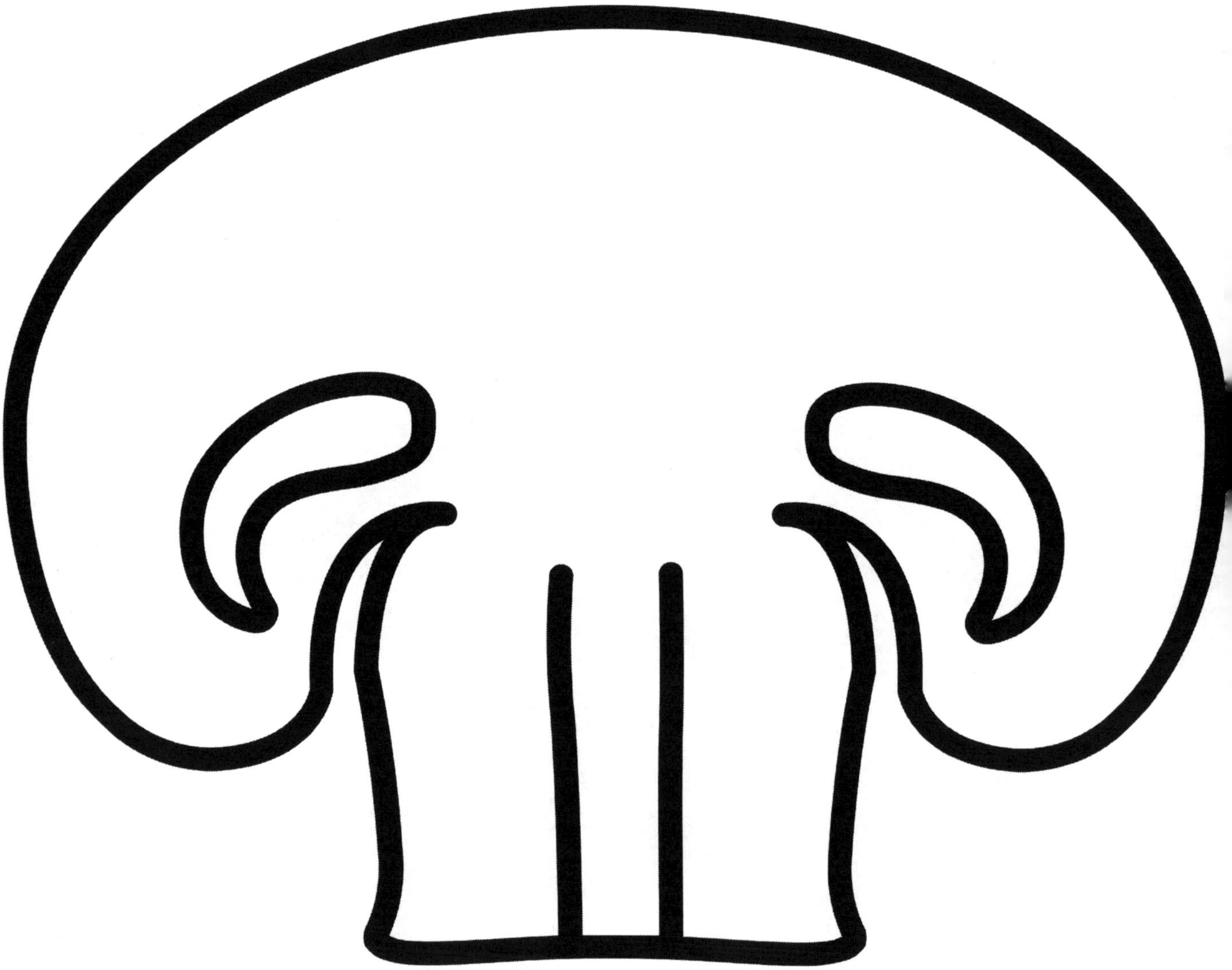

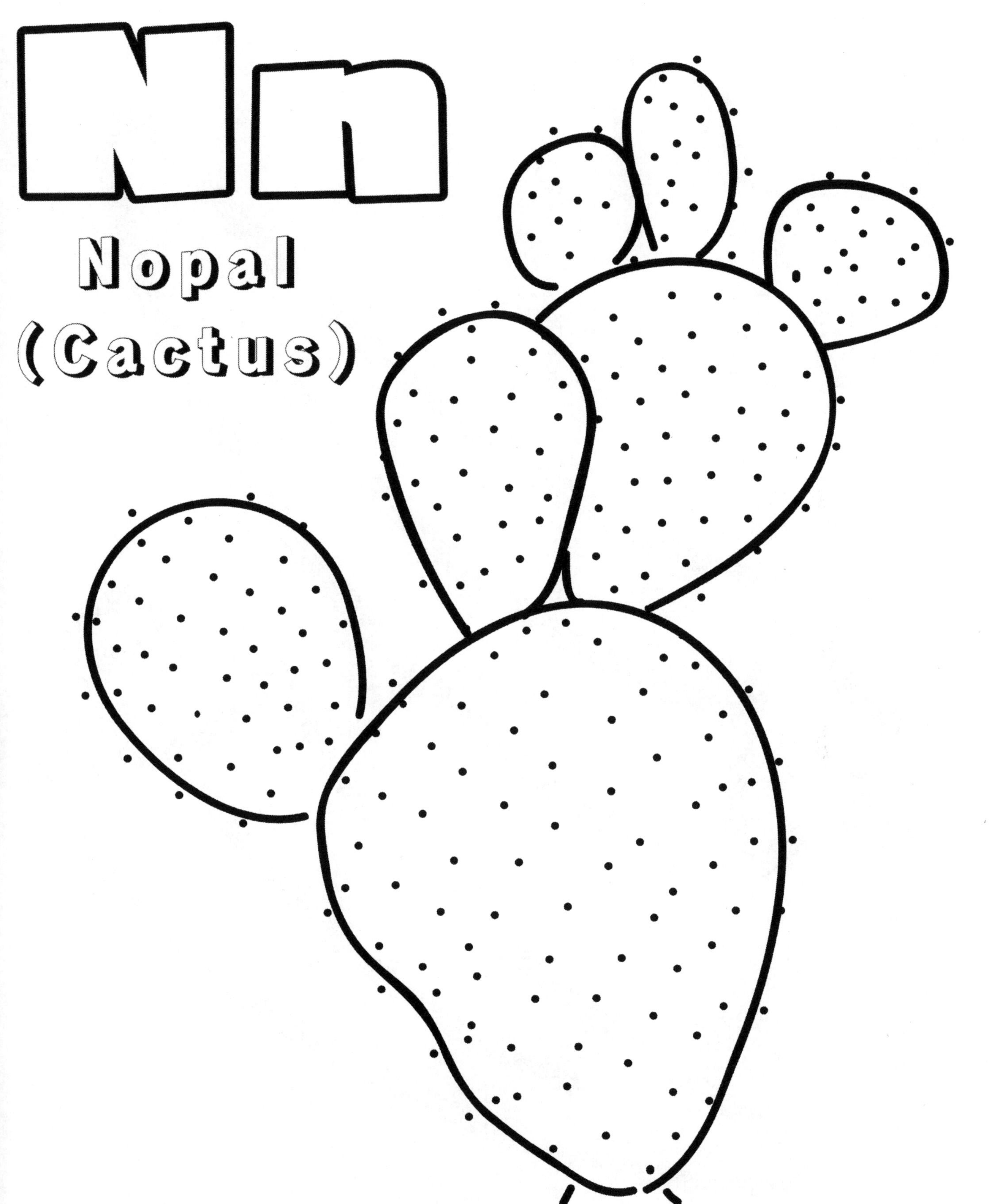
Nn
Nopal
(Cactus)

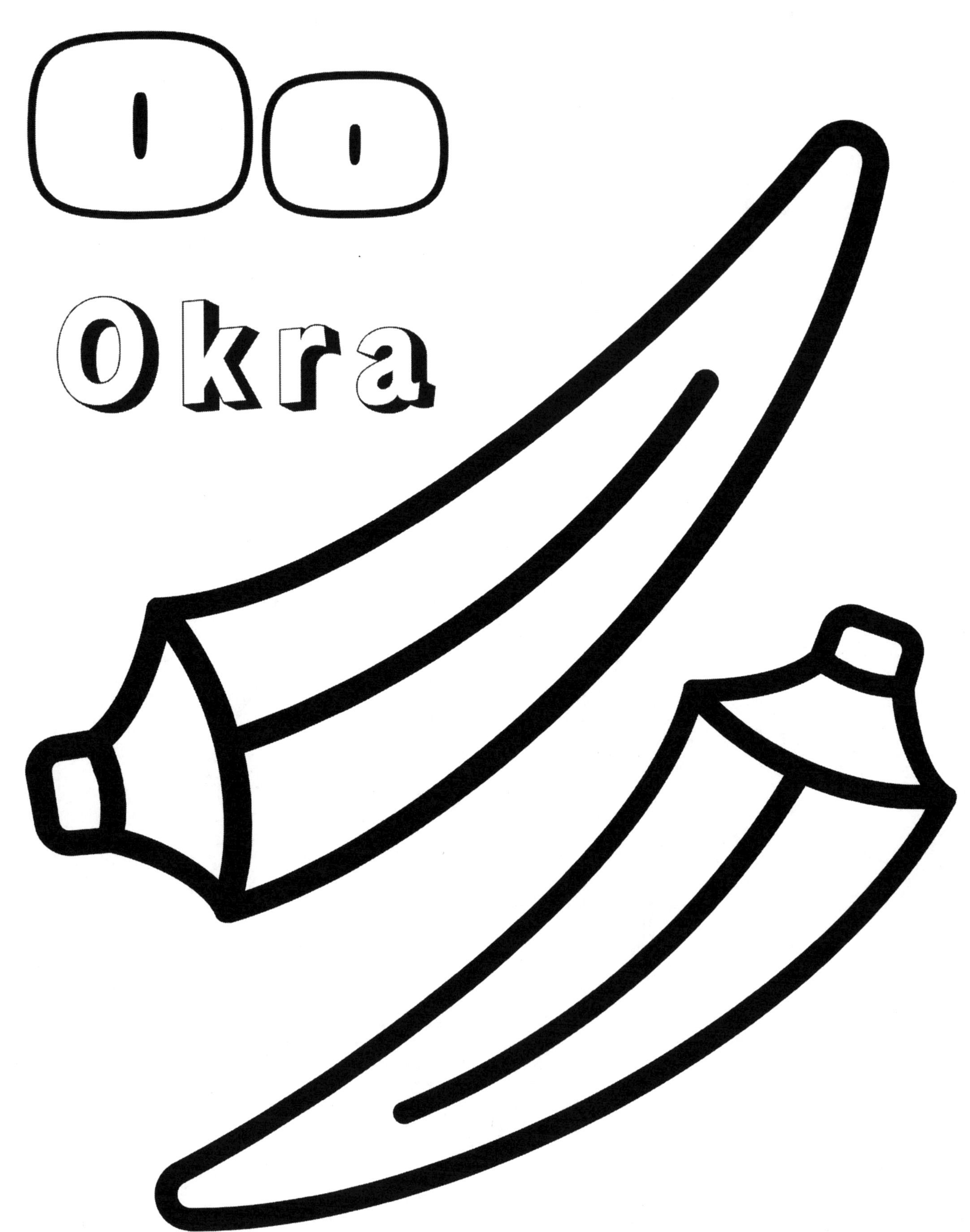
Oo
Okra

Pp Papaya

Qq
Quinoa

Rr

RAW
TAHINI
BUTTER

Ss Soursop

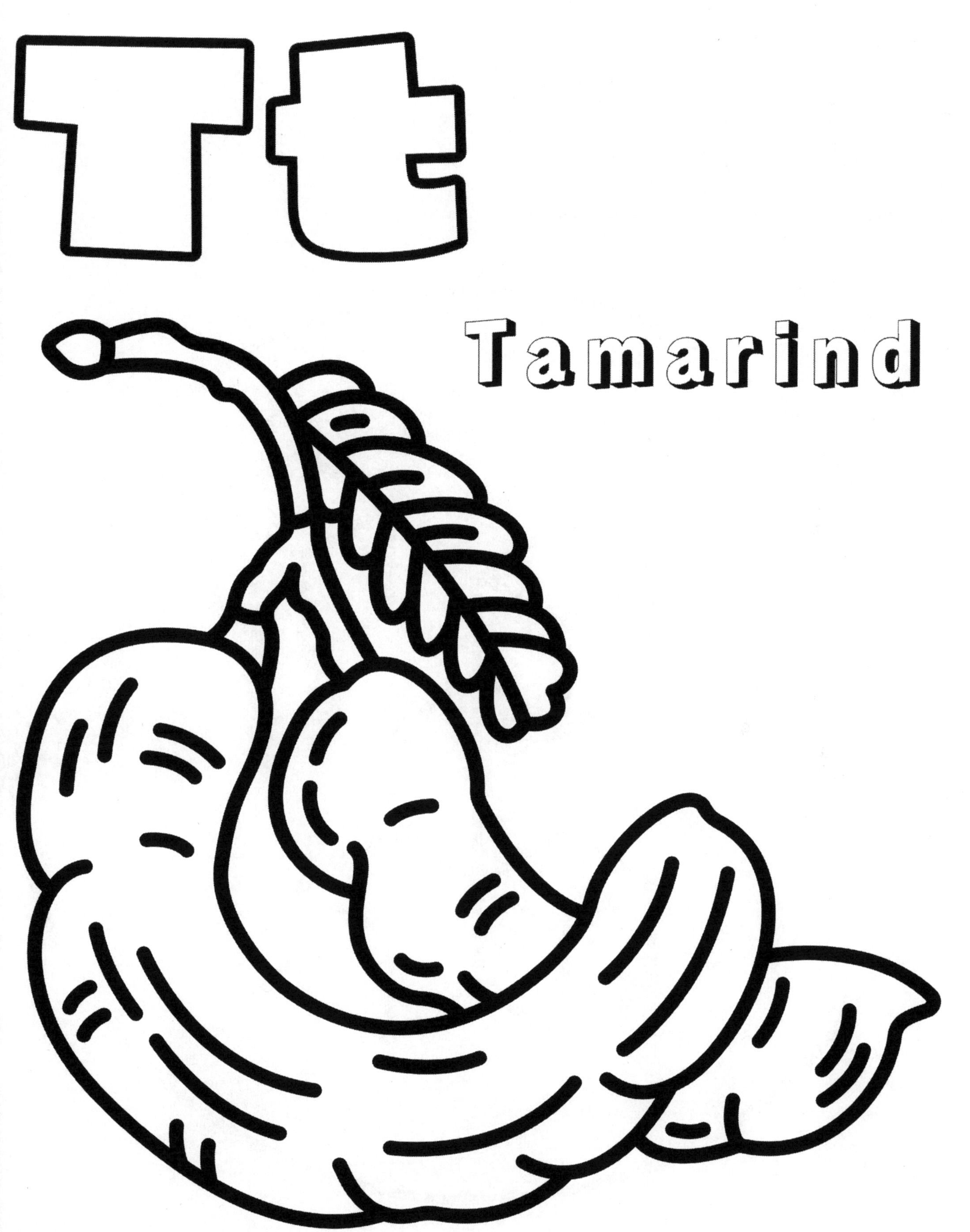
Tt
Tamarind

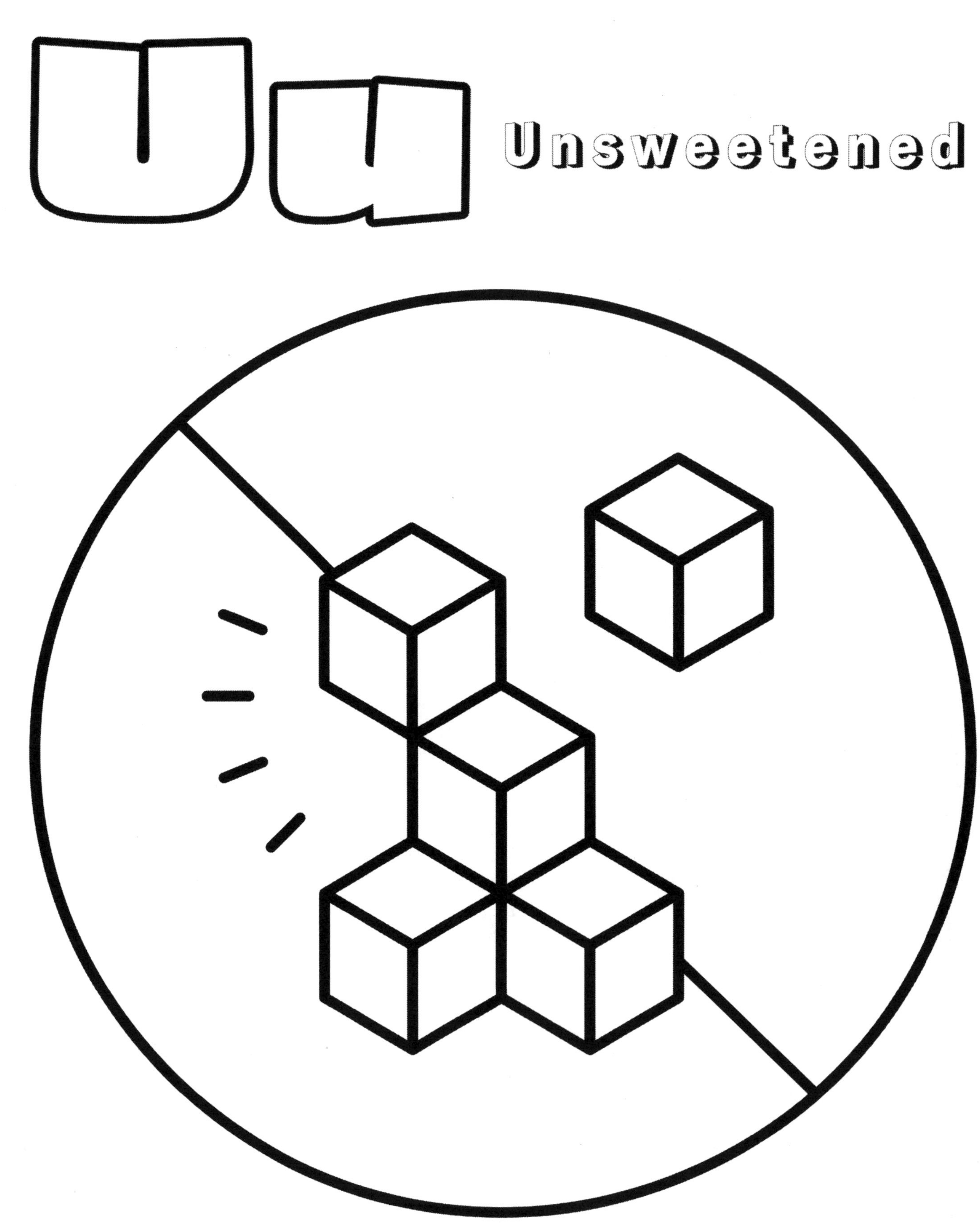
Uu
Unsweetened

Vv

Vegetables (Seeded)

Ww
Watermelon

X x

X-Ray

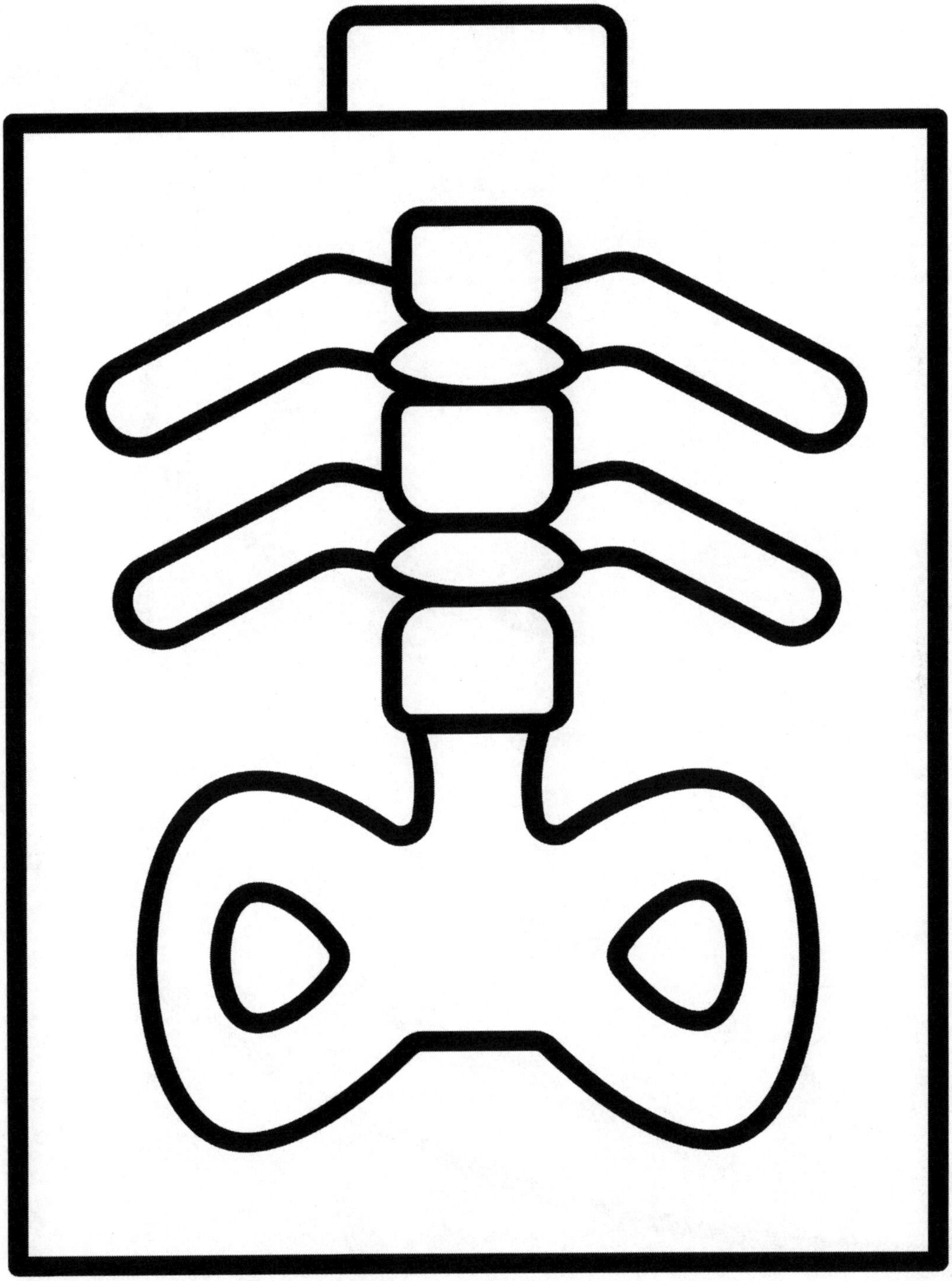

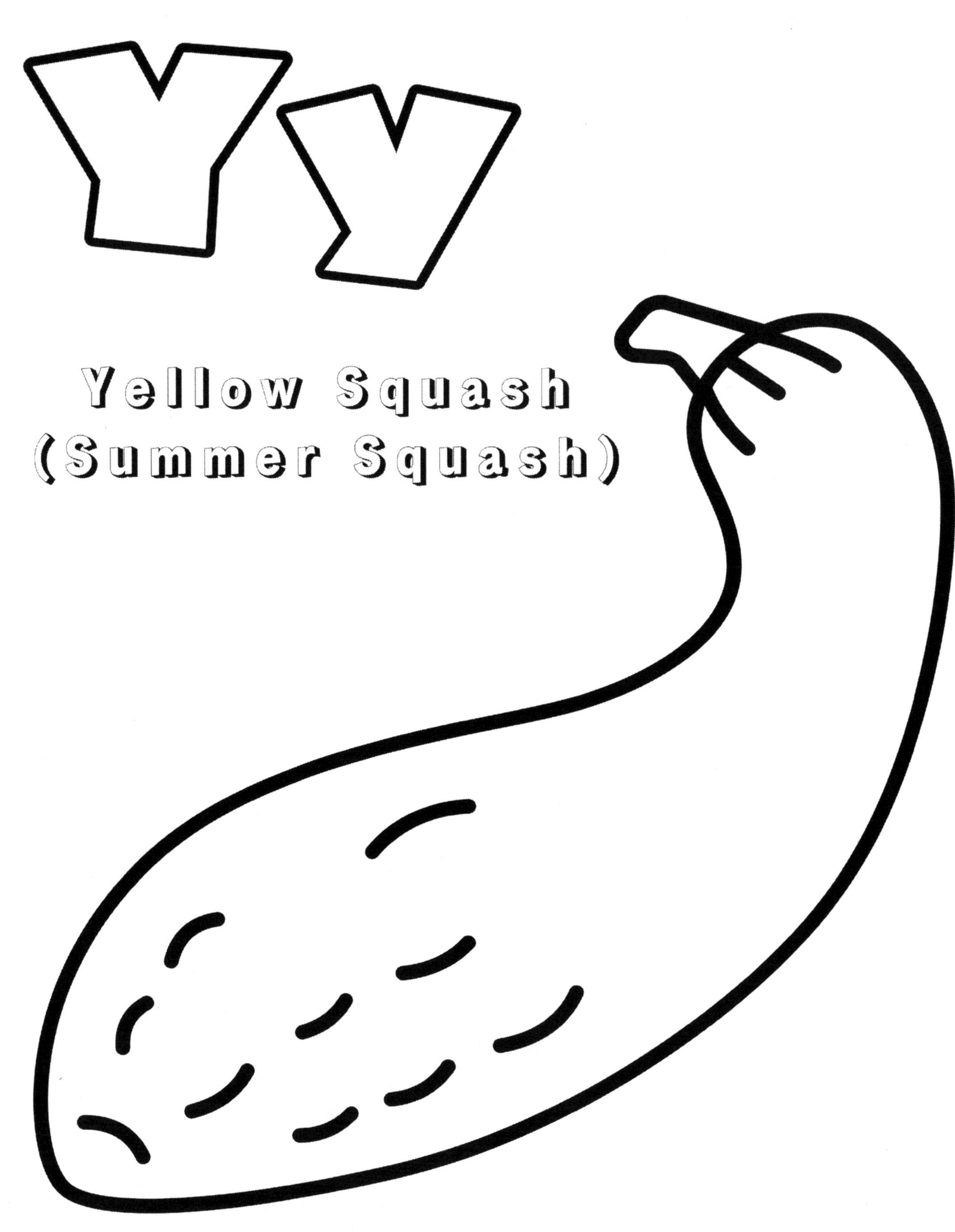
Y y
Yellow Squash
(Summer Squash)

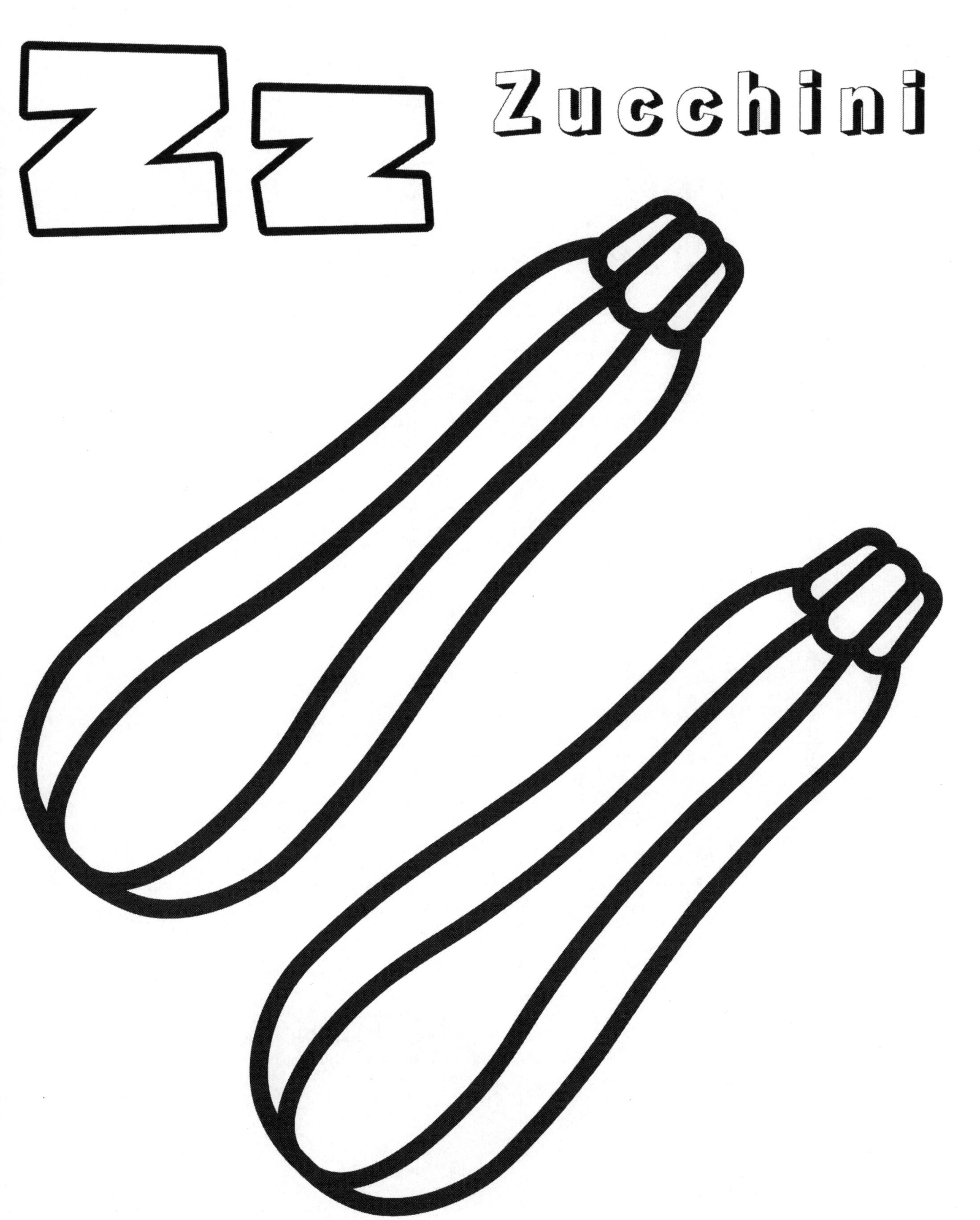
Zz
Zucchini

Made in the USA
Middletown, DE
07 February 2025